This book is dedicated to

_____

and belongs to

_____

Paste picture(s) here

A Book
Extra-illustrated, annotated,
decorated & improved

by

A CAT
NOTEBOOK

AN OLD FASHIONED
KEEPBOOK™

Edited (*before the fact*)
by Linda Campbell Franklin
· · · · ·
Designed (*to be left up to you*)
by Sara Bowman

Tree Communications, Inc.
New York City

© 1982, Tree Communications, Inc. All rights reserved. No part of this work may be reproduced or transmitted in any form by any means, electronic or mechanical, including photocopying and recording, or by any information storage or retrieval system without permission in writing from the publisher.

Published in the United States by Tree Communications, Inc.
250 Park Avenue South
New York City, New York 10003
Printed in the United States of America.
ISBN 0-934504-12-1

This book was typeset in Goudy Old Style by David E. Seham Associates, Inc. Color separations were made by National Colorgraphics, Inc. The paper is 70 lb. Warren Olde Style, cream, supplied by Baldwin Paper Company. The book was printed and bound by R.R. Donnelley & Sons Company.

Many thanks to everyone who worked on this Cat Book, including Shelley Turner, who helped to plan the book, and Carolyn Ogden, who helped make it a reality. I am especially grateful to Felix Farceur, who gave us permission to publish two poems—one of which was written expressly for this book after observing some fancy felines at a show at a Manhattan Savings Bank in New York City.

Cover may be written on with any brand of felt-tip permanent marking pen—bullet- or chiselpoint.

Write us about other books in the Keepbook™ series.

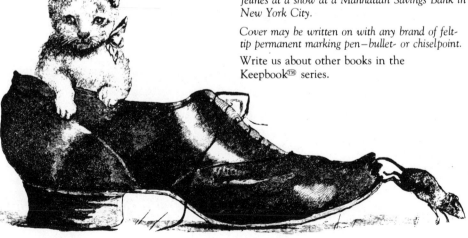

Dear friends,

If you are anything like me, you need a constant supply of notebooks. This Cat Book Keepbook™ is for any cat fancier who fancies a neat and entertaining place in which to scribble notes, copy out poems, draw flowers, press leaves, write a children's story, write a felinography, collect autographs, collect pawprints, keep a diary (52 of the pages are lined), make musical notations, paste in hodgepodges, write down ideas, paste in articles, tape in photographs, stick full of postcards, plan the future, collect favorite recipes, analyze dreams, or anything else you wish. Write your title on the spine with any felt-tipped permanent marking pen. Use the last two pages as an index to the contents: fill in subjects as you go along, or wait until you've finished your book.

Hope you enjoy it!

Yours sincerely,

Linda Campbell Franklin

Hey! diddle, diddle,
The cat and the fiddle,
The cow jumped over the moon;
The little dog laughed to see such sport;
And the dish ran away with the spoon.

Mother Goose

But the kittens were rude and grabbed their food,
and treated the Dolls with jeers;
Which caused their Mother an aching heart
And seven or eight large tears.

From "A Little Girl Asked Some Kittens to Tea," by Joseph Green Francis

10

MR. KATT'S REPLY.

"You're awful stupid,
Mr. Katt—
You're stupid as
can be—
There's lots of
things you
cannot do:
Why, you can't
bark
like
me."

"That's
where you're wrong,"
said Mr. Katt,
His face all
wreathed in
grins,
"Perhaps I cannot
bark like you,
But I often bark my
shins."

From "Little Folks" magazine, October 1916

....

....

....

....

....

....

....

....

....

....

....

....

....

....

....

....

Child & Kitten

"Kitty, Kitty, to scratch is wrong,—
Don't stick out claws so sharp and strong;
I want a paw soft, gentle, and mild."

"Yes, and I'll give you one, dear child;
But it is right that I let you know,
You should not pinch me and beat me so."

If the child pinch'd her by and by,
Hurt poor Kitty, and made her cry;
If Kitty's scratching was not good,
And e'en if it brought a drop of blood,
Neither child nor Kitty did harm intend,
And each continued the other's friend.

From Picture Fables, *poems by F. Hey, 1858*

19

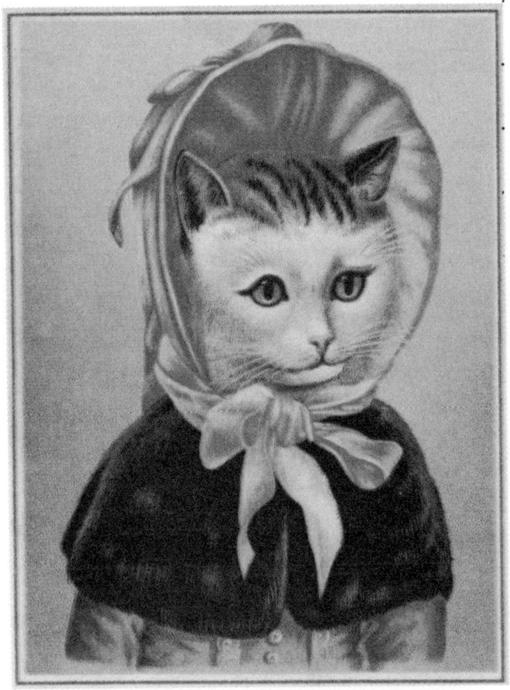

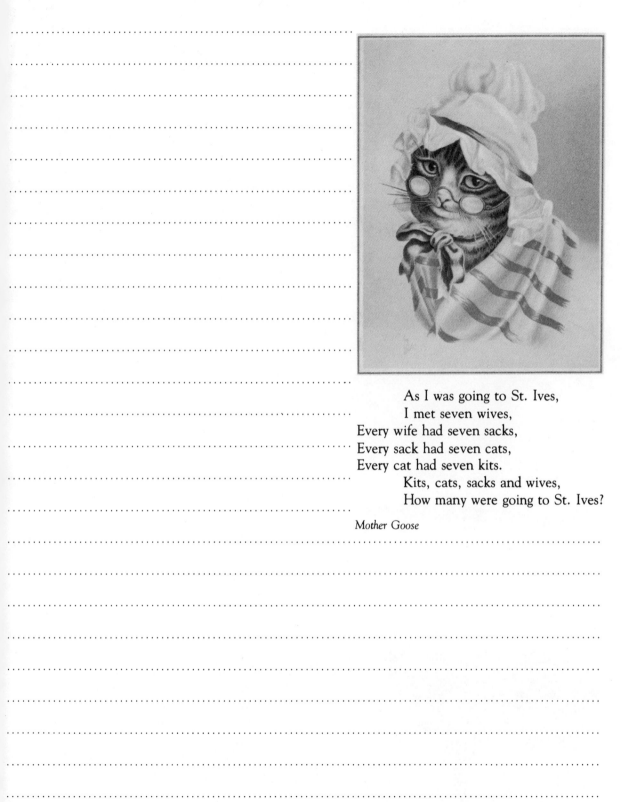

As I was going to St. Ives,
I met seven wives,
Every wife had seven sacks,
Every sack had seven cats,
Every cat had seven kits.
Kits, cats, sacks and wives,
How many were going to St. Ives?

Mother Goose

Her conscious tail her joy declared;
The fair round face, the snowy beard,
   The velvet of her paws,
Her coat, that with the tortoise vies,
Her ears of jet, and emerald eyes,
   She saw, and purred applause.

From "Ode to a Favourite Cat," Thomas Gray

24

"When my cat and I entertain each other with mutual apish tricks, as playing with a garter, who knows but that I make my cat more sport than she makes me? Shall I conclude her to be simple that has her time to begin or to refuse to play, as freely as I myself have? nay, who knows but that it is a defect of my not understanding her language (for doubtless cats talk and reason with one another) that we agree no better; and who knows but that she pities me for being no wiser than to play with her, and laughs and censures my folly for making sport for her when we two play together?"

Miguel de Montaigne

"Keep one eye on the frying-pan, and the other on the cat."

Old Italian proverb

Three little kittens they lost their mittens,
　　And they began to cry,
Oh, mother dear, we sadly fear
　　That we have lost our mittens.
What! lost your mittens, you naughty kittens!
　　Then you shall have no pie.
Mee-ow, mee-ow, mee-ow.
No, you shall have no pie.

The three little kittens they found their mittens,
　　And they began to cry,
Oh, mother dear, see here, see here,
　　For we have found our mittens.
Put on your mittens, you silly kittens,
　　And you shall have some pie.
Purr-r, purr-r, purr-r,
Oh, let us have some pie.

The three little kittens put on their mittens,
　　And soon ate up the pie;
Oh, mother dear, we greatly fear
　　That we have soiled our mittens.
What! soiled your mittens, you naughty kittens!
　　Then they began to sigh,
Mee-ow, mee-ow, mee-ow,
Then they began to sigh.

The three little kittens they washed their mittens,
　　And hung them out to dry;
Oh! mother dear, do you not hear
　　That we have washed our mittens?
What! washed your mittens, then you're good kittens,
　　But I smell a rat close by.
Mee-ow, mee-ow, mee-ow,
We smell a rat close by.

Old nursery rhyme

"Of cats, time does not allow me to say much, but this I must affirm, that they are misrepresented, and often the victims of prejudice. It is strictly maintained that they have little or no affection for *persons,* and that their partialities are confined to *places.* I have known many instances of the reverse. When leaving, about fifteen years ago, a parsonage to remove into Dublin, the cat, that was a favourite with me and with my children, was left behind in our hurry; on seeing strange faces come into the house, she instantly left it, and took up her abode in the top of a very large cabbage-stalk, whose head had been cut off, but which retained a sufficient number of leaves to protect poor puss from the weather; in this position she remained, and nothing could induce her to leave it, until I sent a special messenger to bring her to my house in town."

Reverend Caesar Otway, as quoted in All the Year Round, *June 7, 1862*

"There is a very amusing French fable—*apropos* of instinctive nature—in which a prince falls in love with his cat, and desires a benignant fairy to transform her into a woman. The request is granted; but the palace happening to swarm with mice, the prince's slumbers are disturbed by his bride springing out of bed to go a-mousing, which so disgusts him, that he sees her without regret restored to her original shape."

From Chamber's Journal, *December 26, 1857*

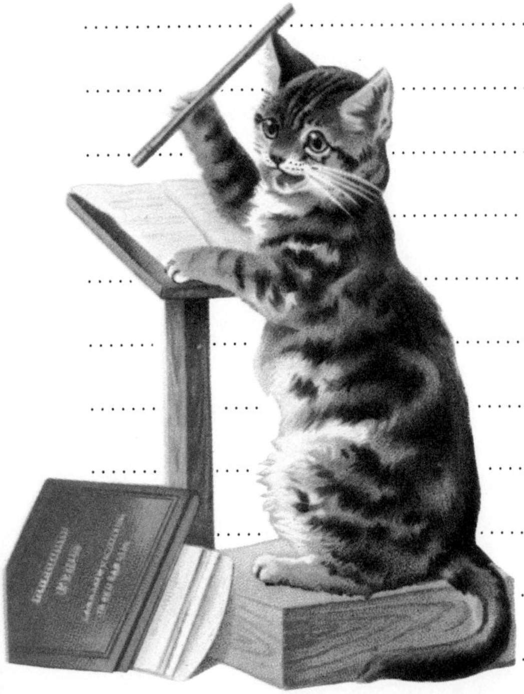

Pussy sits beside the fire,
 So pretty and so fair.
In comes the little Dog,
 Pussy, are you there?
So, so, Mistress Pussy,
 Pray how do you do?
Thank you, thank you, little dog,
 I'm very well just now.

Old nursery rhyme

....

....

....

....

....

....

....

....

....

....

....

....

....

....

....

....

....

....

....

....

....

....

Pussy cat, mew! jumps over a coal
And in her best petticoat burns a great hole.
Pussy cat, mew, shall have no more milk,
Until her best petticoat's mended with silk.

A 16th century nursery rhyme

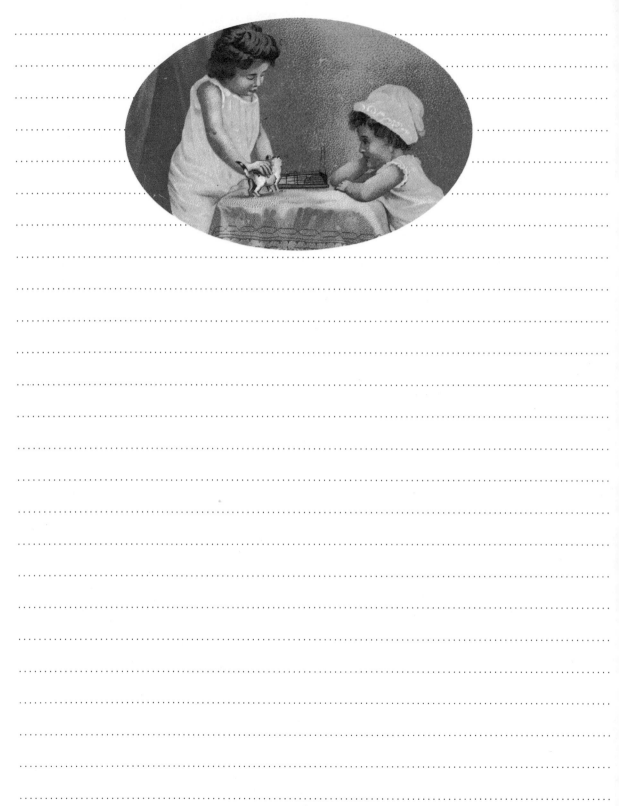

Pat-a-cat, pat-a-cat, as long as you can,
Pat it, and kiss it, and let it lick your hand;
Pat it and tickle it, and listen to it purr,
Keep it in your lap and stroke its fur.

Grace McFarland

Let Hercules himself do what he may,
The cat will mew and dog will have his day.

William Shakespeare, Hamlet

....
....
....
....
....
....
....
....
....
....
....
....
....
....
....
....
....
....
....

My love she is a kitten,
And my heart's a ball of string.

From "My Love and My Heart," by Henry Sambrooke Leigh

....

....

....

....

....

....

....

....

....

....

....

....

....

....

....

....

....

....

....

....

....

"When all candles be out, all cats be gray."

John Heywood, Proverbes

USE NIAGARA STARCH

Cats at Sea

"Considering how much the cat abhors cold water, our readers must often have wondered why seafaring men are so fond of taking the animal with them on a voyage. This is explained by two circumstances. Marine insurance does not cover damage done to cargo by the depredations of rats; but if the owner of the damaged goods can prove that the ship was sent to sea unfurnished with a cat, he can recover damages from the shipmaster. Again, a ship found at sea with no living creature on board is considered a derelict, and is forfeited to the Admiralty, the finders, or the Queen. It has often happened that, after a ship has been abandoned, some domestic animal— a dog, a canary-bird, or most frequently a cat, from its hatred of facing the waves—has saved the vessel from being condemned as a derelict."

From Once a Week, *London, December 26, 1863*

These kittens 'twas said were soon to be wed,
The cards had been out some days,
And cat-birds no doubt spread the news about
As they flew o'er the great high-ways,
And cats, one and all, the great and the small,
Were loud in the kittens' praise.
Miew, miew, miew, miew,
Miew, miew, miew, miew.

....

....

....

....

....

....

....

....

....

....

....

....

....

....

....

....

....

....

....

....

....

The Cats
of Cape Hellini

The cats of Cape Hellini
Gazed upward at the stars
And said, "Who'll be the first of us
To catch a mouse on Mars?"

"We're weary of Chopped Platter
And even Western Dinner,
And do we only think it,
Or are we getting thinner?"

They silently conspired
Each time they sat to stare
As a Cape Hellini rocket
Escaped the atmosphere.

Security was tight
At the Cape Hellini base;
They didn't have a program
For cats in outer space.

The astronauts could go there,
And if they chose came back;
Then the cats of Cape Hellini
Could find a friendly lap

From which to hear the stories
Of the starlight world they craved,
But never got to go
(Though they were well-behaved).

The cats of Cape Hellini
Now stayed up every night
To make their own cat space suits.
They thought, if we're dressed right

They're bound to take us next time;
We already eat dry food,
And pay no mind to gravity.
We really think we could

Be the first of fearless felines
Whose fur would truly fly,
The first intrepid mousers
To mount beyond the sky.

It all looks easy-peasy,
Absolute kitten's-play;
Any cat could learn this stuff
In less than half a day.

So Spot would egg on Annie
And Annie egged on Spot.
They both put on their helmets,
And here's how far they got.

They tip-toed right past ground control,
Across the open space
And loped up to the launch pad
Thinking this must be the place,

When suddenly an astronaut
Who scooped them in his arms
Said, "If you don't tell then I won't tell;
It might set off alarms."

"I'll take you with me just this once,
Your suits are so divine!
Why if I were as small as you,
I'd swap your suit for mine."

They heard the rockets fire,
They felt the thrilling thrust,
And went a million million miles
Past giant lumps of dust.

The mousy-colored planets
Were not composed of mice.
In fact, the cats concluded,
They weren't very nice.

"But we mustn't be ungrateful.
When it's time to meet the press,
We'll call the whole adventure
And unqualified success."

"We're not just pretty faces,
We're not just bits of fluff.
We're sure that if we met Tom Wolfe
He'd say we're the Right Stuff."

The cats of Cape Hellini
Have hung their space boots up;
They reckon that space travel
Of tea is not their cup.

But on a flawless evening,
Admiring the stars,
They say, "It was a pity
About no mice on Mars."

Felix Farceur

The Kittens

Kittens, now I'll find names for you,
Each from the thing it best can do:
Velvet we'll call the one there asleep,
Slyboots the kit who so softly can creep,
Mouser the pussy who hunting doth seem,
Lickdish the one with its nose in the cream.

They grew to be cats, each nice little kit.
Velvet all day on one's lap would sit;
In the corn-loft *Mouser* a-hunting would go,
While *Slyboots* crept through the barn below;
Lickdish went in the kitchen to dwell:
If he was a plague, ask cook,—she'll tell.

From Picture Fables, *poems by F. Hey, 1858*

No cat so sweet a mistress owned;
No mistress owned so sweet a cat.

From "Lapsus Calami," James Kenneth Stephen

The Cat Show Man

The cat show man with the Cheshire smile
Holds cats in the air
And with two hands
Stretches each cat out nearly a mile
And the cat show cats don't care.
The cat show cats are in the know—
Another opening, another show,
Tossed around like pizza dough.
The cat show man shaped like a pear
Twirls the cats up in the air.
(On his loud coat, not one cat hair!)
Now here's a cat he's proud to hold—
A rarity, a Scottish Fold.
He lofts the lop-ear in the air
And bends and flops it here and there.
And do you think this cat would glare?

(His Rarityship does not care.)
The cat show man has cats at home
Who get the best of care,
And people long to touch them
But mostly they don't dare;
Only the cat show man's allowed
To dangle cats in air.
The cats have done their encores,
They haven't turned a hair.
Retired to their cages now,
Collapsed in cat despair,
They start to build the strength back up
To show they do not care.
The cat show man is pleased, pleased, pleased
And beaming everywhere.

Felix Farceur

Reading, Writing and Mieaou-ing

"Cats . . . illustrate a lesson in grammar. The vowel sounds are usually placed in the order a, e, i, o, u, such being their succession in the various alphabets of Europe and Western Asia; but if we wish to place them in that order which marks their relation to one another, we should unite i, e, a, o, u, or in the opposite order, u, o, a, e, i. It has been shown by experiments, that the different vowel sounds may be produced artificially, by throwing a current of air upon a reed in a pipe, and that, as the pipe is lengthened or shortened, the vowels are successively produced in the order above given. When a door creaks, or a cat mews, we have experiments of the same nature, at least as regards the result, for in both cases we may often detect the due series of vowels. Indeed, the word *mew* would be more expressively written *mieaou.* In all these remarks we speak of the vowels as possessing those sounds which are common on the Continent; namely, i like ee, e like ay, a as in father, o as in bone, u as oo, in fool. The reader may try it and say *mi, e, a, o, u,* according to the right way of pronouncing. A little practice, with the help of a cat, will soon make the student perfect."

From "Cat Stories," All the Year Round, A Weekly Journal, conducted by Charles Dickens, London, June 7, 1862

While rain depends, the pensive cat gives o'er
Her frolics, and pursues her tail no more.

From "Description of a City Shower," Jonathan Swift

I love little pussy, her coat is so warm;
And if I don't hurt her she'll do me no harm.
So I'll not pull her tail nor drive her away,
But pussy and I very gently will play.
She shall sit by my side, and I'll give her some food;
And pussy will love me because I am good.

Old nursery rhyme

"What's virtue in man can't be vice in a cat."

From "Both Sides," Mary Abigail Dodge

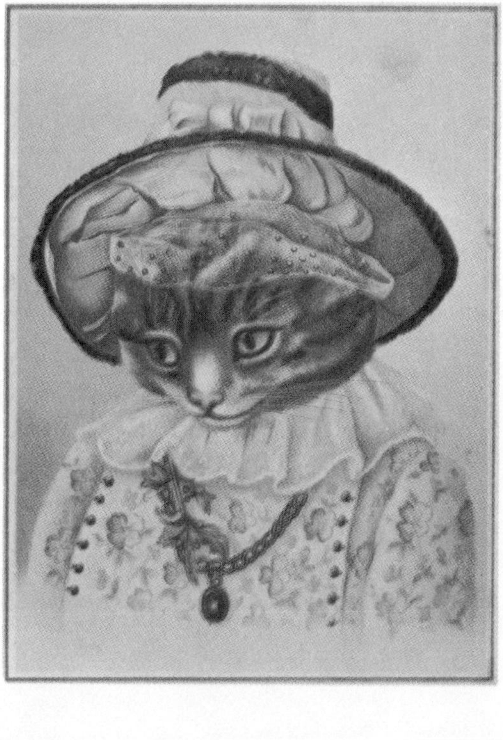

"If cats wore gloves, they would catch no mice."
Old Jewish proverb

THE ARRIVAL

Dandy, the Calico Cat

SOME new people had moved into the [house] next door. They had a little [boy] and a little [girl] and the children liked them very much. But, oh, dear me, they had a big [dog], too! He had a [doghouse] down in the corner of the garden, and he was as gentle as a [lamb], but Dandy was as much afraid of him as if he had been a [lion]. One day when [cat] was hunting for [grasshopper] on his side of the [fence], the big [dog] was gnawing a [bone] on his side. "Bow-wow!" said the big [dog] in his great big voice, and Dandy trembled like a [leaf]. The big [dog] only wanted to play with him, but Dandy did not know it. "Bow-wow!" said the big [dog] again, and came running, and flash! away went [cat] like a streak of [lightning] over the [fence] and down the street. He did not come back the next day or the next, or the next after that. The children cried when they looked at his empty [bowl]. "Dandy is lost," they said. "We shall never see our pet again!"

Then one day Aunt Nell came in with her cheeks as red as [apples]. "I have a new pussy for you, children," she said. "We can never love him as we loved [kitten]!" said Betty. "Oh, I think you will," said [girl]. "I found him behind a [barrel] in the cellar. He must have come in through the [window] in the night. And I have washed him and given him a [bow], and I think you will love him very much." So they all went over to Aunt Nell's [house] that afternoon. You must be as quiet as [mice]," said Aunt Nell, "so as not to frighten the strange new [kitten]. Promise to love him, will you?" "Oh yes, we will," said the children. Then she opened the [door] of her room very softly, and --- Oh, how they jumped and shouted for joy! "Love him! I guess we will! And we will never, never lose him again!" they cried. For the [cat] came running to meet them, and lo, it was not a strange new pussy at all, but Dandy, their own dear, darling, little Calico Cat!

From "Little Folks" magazine, October 1916

*I*ndex

of the Contents

A..

....

....

B..

....

....

C..

....

D..

....

....

E..

....

....

F..

....

....

G..

....

H..

....

I..

....

J..

....

K..

....

L..

....

....

M...

....

....

N...

....

O...

....

....

P...

....

....

Q...

....

....

R...

....

S...

....

....

T...

....

....

U...

....

....

V...

....

W...

....

....

X Y Z...

....

....